GW00858080

Henry's Cat ©
Fun to
Cook Book

Henry's Cat ©
Fun to Cook Book

by Carol Bowen

Dean

First published 1983 by
Deans International Publishing
A Division of The Hamlyn Publishing Group Limited
52-54 Southwark Street, London SE1 1UA

Characters from the Television Series ''Henry's Cat''
© 1983 COPYRIGHT BOB GODFREY FILMS LTD. AND STAN HAYWARD
© 1983 text and artwork DEANS INTERNATIONAL PUBLISHING

All rights reserved. No part of this publication may be
reproduced, stored in a retrieval system, or transmitted
in any form or by any means, electronic, mechanical,
photocopying, recording or otherwise, without the
permission of The Hamlyn Publishing Group Limited
and the copyright holders.

ISBN 0 603 00365 6

Printed in Italy

If you have enjoyed this book and want
to join the Henry's Cat Fan Club, write to:
Henry's Cat Fan Club,
Pippingford Park Manor, Nutley, E. Sussex, England

Contents

Introduction

Henry's Cat enjoys cooking just as much as eating and here are some of his, and his friends most favourite recipes. Throughout the book Henry will show you, step by step, how to make the recipes but before you start, these are his

Rules for the Kitchen

★ Always wear an apron . . . Henry's Cat does.

★ Always wash your hands . . . grey pastry looks weird!

★ Read the recipe all the way through before you start to cook.

★ Collect up all the utensils you will need before starting to cook.

★ Collect and weigh out all the ingredients.

★ Always weigh ingredients accurately. All spoon measures are level *not* heaped ones.

Henry's Cat's Cheesy Grins

Henry's Cat's cheesy grins are delicious cheese nibbles to serve with soups or to eat just on their own.

225 g (8 oz) plain flour
salt and pepper
½ teaspoon mustard powder
50 g (2 oz) butter or margarine
50 g (2 oz) lard
40 g (1½ oz) mature Cheddar cheese, grated
1 tablespoon grated Parmesan cheese
4 tablespoons cold water

You will need...

Makes 24

Say Cheeeese

sieve
mixing bowl
fork
rolling pin
7.5-cm (3-inch) round
  biscuit cutter
knife
baking tray
oven gloves
spatula
cooling rack

1 Sift the flour, a little salt and pepper and the mustard powder into the bowl.

2 Rub in the butter or margarine and the lard with your fingertips until the mixture resembles fine breadcrumbs. Add the water and mix with a fork to a smooth dough.

COUGH!

3 Roll out the pastry on a lightly-floured surface using a floured rolling pin to 0.5 cm ($\frac{1}{4}$ inch) thickness. With the cutter, cut out as many rounds as possible, re-rolling where necessary.

4 Cut each round in half with a knife. Make a small slit across each semi-circle and open out the pastry to make a smiling mouth.

5 Place on a greased baking tray and bake in an oven preheated to moderately hot (200°C, 400°F, Gas Mark 6) for about 10 minutes until golden. Use a spatula to move them to a cooling rack.

13

Mosey Mouse's Whiskers

Mosey Mouse's Whiskers are delicious savoury biscuits coated with a few crunchy poppy seeds.

75 g (3 oz) wholemeal flour
15 g ($\frac{1}{2}$ oz) medium oatmeal
pinch of salt
40 g ($1\frac{1}{2}$ oz) lard
$1\frac{1}{2}$ teaspoons brown sugar
20 g ($\frac{3}{4}$ oz) Cheshire cheese, grated
1 small egg, beaten
1-2 teaspoons water
poppy seeds

mixing bowl
spoon
fork
rolling pin
knife
pastry brush
baking tray
spatula
oven gloves
cooling rack

You will need...

Makes about 25

1 Mix the flour with the oatmeal and salt in the bowl. Stir in the sugar and cheese, mixing well.

2 Add about two-thirds of the egg and water and mix with a fork to a smooth dough.

Have I got a SURPRISE for Mosey Mouse!

What are you cooking today, Henry's Cat?

What did Mosey Mouse say when when he broke his teeth?   HARD CHEESE!

14

3 Roll out on a lightly-floured surface with a floured rolling pin to 0.5 cm ($\frac{1}{4}$ inch) thickness. Cut out as many strips measuring 7.5 × 1 cm (3 × $\frac{1}{2}$ inch) as possible.

4 Brush one end of each strip with a little of the remaining egg, then dip in poppyseeds to coat.

5 Pinch three strips of pastry together at the uncoated ends to form three whiskers. Dampen the end with water and join two sets of whiskers together to make a complete set of six. Place on a greased baking tray.

6 Bake in an oven preheated to moderate (180°C, 350°F, Gas Mark 4) for about 15 minutes until lightly golden. Use a spatula to remove them to a cooling rack.

15

Lion Pizzas

Henry's Cat has dedicated these tasty pastry pizzas to his cousin the lion since they easily cope with man-sized appetites!

100 g (4 oz) plain flour
pinch of salt
25 g (1 oz) butter or margarine
25 g (1 oz) lard
40 g (1½ oz) Cheddar cheese, grated
2 tablespoons cold water
1 (398-g/14-oz) can peeled tomatoes, drained
75 g (3 oz) cooked ham, finely chopped
1 (225-g/8-oz) can baked beans in tomato sauce

24 black olives
few anchovy fillets

You will need...

Makes 8

sieve
2 mixing bowls
fork
rolling pin
10-cm (4-inch) round cutter
baking tray
spoon
knife
oven gloves

1 Sift the flour and salt into a bowl. Rub in the butter or margarine and lard with your fingertips until the mixture resembles fine breadcrumbs. Add the water and mix with a fork to a smooth dough.

2 Roll out the pastry on a lightly-floured surface using a floured rolling pin to 0.5 cm (¼ inch) thickness. With the cutter, cut out 8 (10-cm/4-inch) rounds, re-rolling where necessary. Place on a greased baking tray.

Hare Pussy Pussy

This is Henry's Cat's favourite main meal, a slow-cooking casserole with hare and vegetables.
If you don't like hare then you can use rabbit or chicken instead.

350 g (12 oz) hare, rabbit or chicken, boned
  and chopped
2 parsnips, peeled and sliced
2 carrots, peeled and sliced
1 onion, peeled and sliced
2 sticks celery, scrubbed and sliced
1 (298-g/10½-oz) can condensed chicken,
  tomato or vegetable soup
4 tablespoons cold water
1 teaspoon mixed dried herbs
100 g (4 oz) button mushrooms
100 g (4 oz) frozen peas

You will need...

1 medium-sized casserole with lid
spoon
can opener
oven gloves

Serves 2-3

or just Henry's Cat

NOT likely...

1 Place the hare, rabbit or chicken in the casserole dish with the parsnip, carrot, onion and celery.

Shall I use rabbit today...

...or chicken?

HOW TO COOK VEGETABLES by R T Choke

2 Spoon over the condensed and undiluted soup. Add the water and sprinkle over the herbs.

Wonder what's bothering Chris Rabbit?

3 Cover and cook in an oven preheated to moderate (180°C, 350°F, Gas Mark 4) for 1½ hours.

Time for a nap.

ZZZZZZ

CAT NAP

4 Remove from the oven with gloves and carefully remove the lid. Add the mushrooms and peas and stir well.

*You could tell if it was rabbit stew from the hares in it!

5 Cover and return to the oven. Cook for a further 30 minutes. Serve the casserole hot.

Hope you enjoy it, Chris Rabbit.

Smells good!

Close shave!

19

Curly Quiche

This is Henry's Cat's idea of a bit of fun – a lovely pastry quiche with a long curly sausage that looks like Douglas Dog's tail.

For the pastry:
225 g (8 oz) plain flour
salt and pepper
50 g (2 oz) butter or margarine
50 g (2 oz) lard
2 tablespoons cold water
For the filling:
1 (400-g/14-oz) packet Cumberland
   sausage
2 eggs
150 ml (¼ pint) milk

You will need...

sieve
2 mixing bowls
fork
rolling pin
1 (23-cm/9-inch) flan dish
   or tin
egg whisk
oven gloves

Serves 6

1 Sift the flour and a pinch of salt into the mixing bowl. Rub in the butter or margarine and lard with your fingertips until the mixture resembles fine breadcrumbs. Add the water and mix to a smooth dough with a fork.

...but Henry's Cat and Douglas Dog will have half each.

Douglas Dog's tail inspired this quiche.

2 Roll out the pastry on a lightly-floured surface to make a circle large enough to line the flan dish. Carefully lift the pastry onto the rolling pin and unroll over the dish. Press into the sides and roll the rolling pin over the top to remove the excess pastry.

3 Arrange the Cumberland sausage in a spiral like a curly dog's tail on the base of the flan.

4 Beat the eggs in a bowl with the milk and salt and pepper to taste. Carefully pour into the flan.

5 Bake in an oven preheated to moderately hot (190°c, 375°f, Gas Mark 5) for 35-40 minutes or until golden brown and firm. Serve hot or cold.

"A proud moment for Douglas Dog."

Henry's Cat's Toadstools

Henry's Cat hasn't found fairies at the bottom of the garden but he's found their toadstools in the kitchen!

4 hard-boiled eggs, shelled
1 (115-g/4¼-oz) can sardines in tomato
  sauce
2 tablespoons salad cream
1 teaspoon snipped chives
salt and pepper
4 large tomatoes
shredded lettuce
2 tablespoons cheese spread

knife
chopping board
spoon
mixing bowl
teaspoon
plate
skewer

Serves 4

You will need...

What's Phillipe Frog's favourite flower?

A croakus

1 Cut the eggs in half crossways and scoop out the yolks into a mixing bowl.

2 Add the sardines, salad cream, chives and salt and pepper to taste. Mix well to blend.

Have you heard the joke about the eggs?

NO!

Too bad...

I'll save one or two for a late-night snack...

3 Using a teaspoon, fill the egg white hollows with the sardine mixture. Place cut side down on a serving plate. Cut a thin slice of egg white from the top of each egg to make a flat platform.

4 Cut the tomatoes in half and balance one tomato half on top of each egg half to make 'toadstools'. Fill any space between the toadstools with shredded lettuce.

5 Using cheese spread straight from the tube, squeeze out small dots of cheese over the tomato halves. If your spread comes in a jar or packet use a skewer to make these dots. Serve at once.

Anyone for Leap Frog?

23

Beefburger Nests

Worth climbing up a tree for, Henry's Cat's Beefburger Nests are delicious beefburgers with a crispy potato and egg topping.

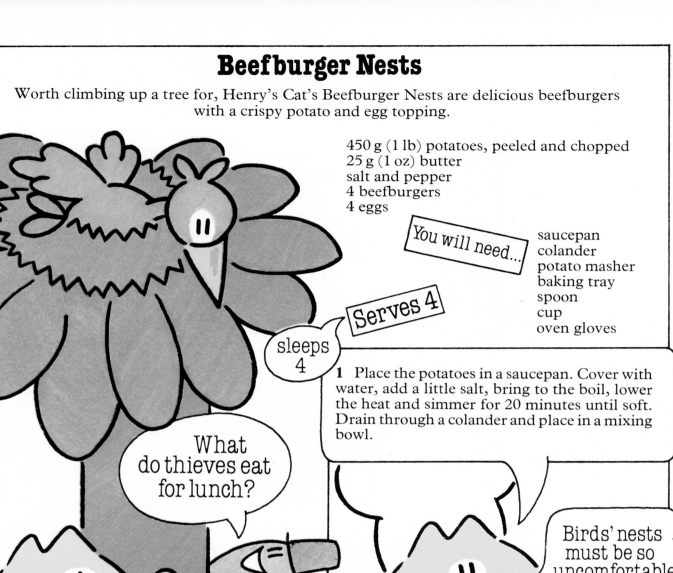

450 g (1 lb) potatoes, peeled and chopped
25 g (1 oz) butter
salt and pepper
4 beefburgers
4 eggs

You will need...
saucepan
colander
potato masher
baking tray
spoon
cup
oven gloves

Serves 4

sleeps 4

What do thieves eat for lunch?

1 Place the potatoes in a saucepan. Cover with water, add a little salt, bring to the boil, lower the heat and simmer for 20 minutes until soft. Drain through a colander and place in a mixing bowl.

Birds' nests must be so uncomfortable.

2 Add the butter and salt and pepper to taste and mash until smooth.

3 Place the beefburgers on the baking tray. Spoon the potato evenly on top of the beefburgers right to the edges. Make a hollow in the middle of each with the back of a spoon.

4 Break the eggs individually into a cup and tip one into each of the 'nests'.

5 Bake in an oven preheated to moderately hot (200°C, 400°F, Gas Mark 6) for 20 minutes until the potato is golden and the egg has just set.

Cat's Tongue

This isn't really a cat's tongue but Henry's Cat's way of serving a savoury bean mixture in a long French loaf like a cat's tongue.

1 stubby French loaf
1 (450-g/15.9-oz) can baked beans in
 tomato sauce
73 g (3 oz) cooked ham, finely chopped
4 tablespoons sage and onion stuffing mix
salt and pepper

knife
chopping board
mixing bowl
spoon
foil
oven gloves

You will need...

Serves 4

or ONE FRENCHMAN THINLY DISGUISED AS H.C.

1 Cut a thin slice from each end of the French loaf and carefully hollow out all the white breadcrumbs (use for another dish).

2 Mix the beans in the mixing bowl with the ham, stuffing mix and salt and pepper to taste. Leave the mixture to stand for 30 minutes.

This time can be best spent...
...having...
snooze"...

3 Spoon and pack the bean mixture into the bread hollow. Replace the 'ends' and wrap in foil to completely enclose.

4 Bake in an oven preheated to moderately hot (190°C, 375°F, Gas Mark 5) for 15 minutes.

Ohh la la!

← A French Bean!

Suppose I'd better wash-up while it's cooking.

5 Remove from the oven and slice into rounds to serve.

Très bon n'est-ce pas!

What's French and very restful?

A long loaf!

Definitely ESCARGOTS next...

Fish Cakes

Henry's Cat loves fish in his dish and these delicious treats are fish shaped too!

175 g (6 oz) potatoes, peeled and chopped
salt and pepper
100 g (4 oz) cod
15 g (½ oz) butter
2 teaspoons chopped parsley
flour to coat
1 small egg, beaten
golden or toasted breadcrumbs
150 ml (¼ pint) cooking oil
4 small parsley sprigs

2 saucepans
colander
mixing bowl
potato masher
knife
2 plates
frying pan
spatula
absorbent kitchen paper

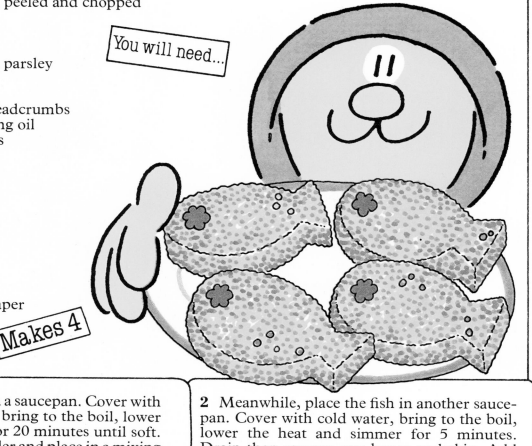

You will need...

Makes 4

1 Place the potatoes in a saucepan. Cover with water, add a little salt, bring to the boil, lower the heat and simmer for 20 minutes until soft. Drain through a colander and place in a mixing bowl.

2 Meanwhile, place the fish in another saucepan. Cover with cold water, bring to the boil, lower the heat and simmer for 5 minutes. Drain then remove any bones and skin. Add the fish to the potatoes in the mixing bowl.

3 Add the butter, parsley and salt and pepper to taste to the potato mixture and mash until smooth.

4 Turn onto a floured surface and shape into a roll with your hands. Cut into four thick slices and shape each slice into a fish shape.

Fish & ships!

5 Place the egg on one plate and the breadcrumbs on another. Dip the fish cakes in the egg to coat well and then into the breadcrumbs, pressing the breadcrumbs onto the fish.

6 Heat the oil in the frying pan. Add the fish cakes and cook gently for 10 minutes until golden underneath. Turn over with a spatula and cook on the other side until golden. Drain on kitchen paper. Press a parsley sprig into each fish cake to make the 'eye'. Serve at once.

29

Hot Diggerty Dogs

Henry's Cat usually stays well clear of dogs, except Douglas, but not these scrumptious frankfurter ones!

4 frankfurter sausages
1 (142-g/5-oz) can baked beans in tomato
  sauce
2 tablespoons brown sauce
4 long soft bread rolls

2 saucepans
spoon
knife
breadboard
colander
4 paper napkins

You will need...

Serves 4

or ONE hungry dog...

I'm going to help Henry's Cat today...

...I'm feeling peckish.

1 Bring a saucepan of water to the boil. Add the frankfurters and cook for 5 minutes.

2 Meanwhile, place the beans in another saucepan with the brown sauce. Heat gently until hot, about 5 minutes.

You can heat the beans...

What did the frankfurter say to the beans Douglas Dog?

DUNNO

That's enough of your sauce... HA... HA!

3 Make a lengthways slit in each bread roll with a knife.

4 Drain the frankfurters in a colander.

5 Place a frankfurter in each roll and top with a good spoonful of the bean mixture. Serve the Hot Diggerty Dogs wrapped in paper napkins.

Pansy Pig's Crispy Egg Boats

Pansy Pig is always on a diet but she loves these naughty-cal treats!

8 crispbreads
butter to spread
4 hard-boiled eggs, shelled
2 tablespoons mayonnaise
salt and pepper
2 tomatoes, quartered and seeded

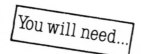
You will need...

mixing bowl
knife
chopping board
spoon
8 cocktail sticks

Serves 4

or ONE PANSY PIG on a diet!

32

1 Lightly spread the crispbreads with butter.

2 Chop the eggs on a chopping board with a knife then place in a mixing bowl. Add the mayonnaise and salt and pepper to taste and mix well with a spoon.

3 Spoon and spread evenly on top of the crispbreads.

4 Push a cocktail stick through each tomato quarter and position each on the crispbread boat to make a 'sail'.

33

Toasted Welsh Catbits

This recipe came from Henry's Cat's Welsh cousin and is all the more delicious since it contains fish as well as cheese.

50 g (2 oz) canned sardines, drained
½ teaspoon Worcestershire sauce
¼ small cucumber, very finely chopped
½ small red pepper, finely chopped
½ teaspoon vinegar
salt and pepper
1 tablespoon mayonnaise
4 slices wholemeal bread, toasted
50 g (2 oz) cheese, grated

mixing bowl
fork
spoon
knife
oven gloves

You will need...

Serves 4

1 Place the sardines, Worcestershire sauce, cucumber, pepper, vinegar and salt and pepper to taste in a bowl. Mash with a fork.

My Welsh cousin, Dai Mog is a terrific cook...

Why is Wales a wet country?   Because it has lots of leeks!

2 Add the mayonnaise and stir well. Spoon the fish mixture evenly over the slices of toast and sprinkle with the cheese.

What's brown on both sides and 190m high? THE TOAST OFFICE TOWER.

3 Place the toasts on a grill rack in a grill pan. Toast under a hot grill until golden and bubbly, about 4-5 minutes.

4 Remove from the grill and allow to cool slightly before cutting into triangles to serve.

Henry's Cat's Chocolate Mice

Henry's Cat likes to eat mice and these chocolate ones are extra delicious!

small knob of butter
1 tablespoon cocoa powder
2 tablespoons hot water
75 g (3 oz) icing sugar, sifted
1 packet marshmallows
8 chocolate cup cakes
1 small packet chocolate buttons
little chocolate spread
16 currants
2 glacé cherries, quartered
thin strips of liquorice

You will need...

small saucepan
wooden spoon
knife
skewer

Makes 8

Enough for a tea party

1 Make the icing by melting the butter in a small saucepan. Add the cocoa powder, water and icing sugar. Mix to a smooth paste.

2 Dip the marshmallows in the icing and stick one on top of each cup cake. Leave until set.

3 Make two small slits, using a hot knife, in the top of each marshmallow and stick in two buttons to make 'ears'.

I'm inviting ALL my friends to tea.

If you cross a small furry animal with a cocoa bean do you get a chocolate mousse?

36

4 Carefully dot small pieces of chocolate spread on each marshmallow to make the 'eyes' and 'nose'. Press two currants on to the spread for the 'eyes' and a piece of cherry for the 'nose'.

5 Make a hole in the back of each marshmallow with a hot skewer and push in a strip of liquorice for the 'tail'.

Ginger Toms

Henry's Cat doesn't like any other cat on his patch – except these tasty Ginger Toms!

150 g (5 oz) plain flour
1½ teaspoons ground ginger
½ teaspoon ground mixed spice
2 tablespoons golden syrup
25 g (1 oz) butter
2 tablespoons castor sugar
½ teaspoon bicarbonate of soda
1 small egg, beaten
30 currants
strips of angelica

You will need...

baking tray   oven gloves
sieve   spatula
mixing bowl   cooling rack
wooden spoon
small saucepan
rolling pin
7.5-cm (3-inch) round biscuit
   cutter

Makes 10

1 Grease the baking tray. Sift the flour, ginger and mixed spice into a bowl.

2 Place the golden syrup, butter and sugar in the saucepan and heat until melted. Add to the flour mixture with the bicarbonate of soda and egg and mix with a wooden spoon to a soft dough.

3 Roll out the dough on a lightly-floured surface to a 0.5 cm (¼ inch) thickness using a floured rolling pin.

4 Cut out rounds with the biscuit cutter until all the dough has been used. Carefully pinch the top of each round in two places to make 'ears' for the cats.

5 Press three currants on each for the 'eyes' and 'nose'. Press a few strips of angelica either side of the 'nose' to make the 'whiskers'.

6 Bake in an oven preheated to moderate (190°C, 375°F, Gas Mark 5) for 10 minutes until pale golden brown. Use a spatula to move them to a cooling rack.

Rocking Chair Trifles

Henry's Cat devised this recipe while day dreaming one day in his cat basket – it has a mouth-watering cushion of sponge underneath the fruit, custard and cream.

4 trifle sponges
2 tablespoons raspberry jam
175 g (6 oz) raspberries, strawberries or
  other fresh or canned fruit
4 tablespoons undiluted blackcurrant
  cordial
4 egg yolks
50 g (2 oz) castor sugar
3 tablespoons cornflour
600 ml (1 pint) milk
300 ml ($\frac{1}{2}$ pint) whipped cream

knife
4 paper trifle cases
saucepan
wooden spoon
spoon

1 Slice the trifle sponges in half and sandwich together again with the jam. Place the sponges evenly in the trifle cases. Top with the fruit and blackcurrant cordial, saving a few pieces of fruit to decorate.

2 Mix the egg yolks, sugar and cornflour in a saucepan with the wooden spoon. Gradually add the milk, mixing well.

3 Slowly bring to the boil, stirring all the time. When boiling cook for 2-3 minutes, still stirring. Remove from the heat, allow to cool a little then pour over the sponge and fruit mixture. Chill until lightly set.

4 Swirl the cream on top of the trifles and decorate with the reserved pieces of fruit.

mm
mmmooo
mmm

I said she could share the Trifle... ...NOT my Rocking Chair!

Nine Lives Syllabub

This delicious creamy dessert won't separate or collapse like the traditional syllabub – it literally has nine lives and can be kept in the refrigerator until required.

150 ml (¼ pint) lemon curd
150 ml (¼ pint) apple juice
300 ml (½ pint) double cream
12 sponge fingers

mixing bowl
whisk
spoon
6 dessert glasses

You will need...

Serves 6

1 Place the lemon curd, apple juice and double cream in the bowl.

2 Whisk with the rotary beater until very thick.

3 Spoon into the dessert glasses and chill until required.

4 Just before serving top each syllabub with two sponge fingers.

What do you call a cat who sucks lemons? Sour puss!

Henry's Cat's Express

This is Henry's Cat's favourite birthday type cake that is really easy to make.

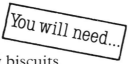

You will need...

2 loaf shaped cakes
1 small packet Maltesers
1 packet chocolate fingers
1 packet chocolate marshmallow biscuits
a little whipped cream
few Smarties to decorate

knife
serving plate
spoon
round cutter

Serves 8-10

1 Using a knife, carefully cut an oblong out of one of the cakes, about 2.5 cm (1 inch) from the edge, and almost through to the base. Remove the cut piece of cake in one piece. Cut to make the train's high front carriage and funnel as below.

2 Fill the hollowed out cake with the cargo of Maltesers and chocolate fingers.

3 Place the two cakes on a serving plate and place chocolate marshmallow biscuits around the cakes to make the 'wheels'.

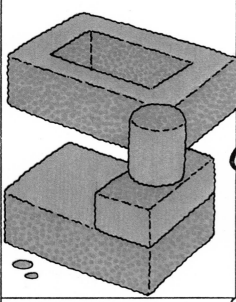

4 Swirl a little cream on the funnel to make the steam and decorate the carriage with Smarties. Slice to serve.

43

Henry's Cat's Rosy Cooler

Henry's Cat is a real cool cat but when he gets a little hot under the collar this is his favourite cool drink.

12 ice cubes
350 ml (12 fl oz) unsweetened pineapple
   juice, chilled
350 ml (12 fl oz) unsweetened orange juice,
   chilled
2 tablespoons grenadine or raspberry syrup
4 slices orange
8 glacé cherries

You will need...

4 tall glasses
jug
4 cocktail sticks

Serves 4

1 Place three ice cubes in the bottom of each glass.

2 Pour the pineapple and orange juices evenly between the glasses.

3 Pour a thin dribble of grenadine or raspberry syrup in a circle around the top edge of the drinks. It will sink to give a rosy layer at the bottom of the glasses.

4 Thread an orange slice and a glacé cherry on each cocktail stick and balance across the top of each glass to serve.

45

Cat's Eyes

These are delicious apples stuffed with dried fruit and coconut and topped with a sweet cat's eye!

4 medium dessert apples
50 g (2 oz) sultanas
25 g (1 oz) desiccated coconut
1 tablespoon clear honey
1 tablespoon brown sugar
8 coloured glacé cherries

You will need...

apple corer
knife
chopping board
mixing bowl
spoon
large oval ovenproof dish
oven gloves

Serves 4

What's green, bad tempered and good with custard?

Apple Grumble

1 Carefully core the centre of the apples. Slice the apples in half crossways.

2 Mix the sultanas with the coconut, honey and brown sugar.

3 Place the apple halves cut sides down in the ovenproof dish. Spoon the fruit mixture into the centre hole of each.

4 Bake in an oven preheated to moderately hot (200°C, 400°F, Gas Mark 6) for 30-40 minutes until tender. Serve at once each apple half topped with a coloured glacé cherry to make the cat's eyes.

Henry's Cat's Arctic Igloos

Both hot and cold these desserts are Henry's Cat's choice when you can't make up your mind which you would prefer.

4 egg whites
225 g (8 oz) castor sugar
1 ice cream and sponge Arctic roll
4 slices canned pineapple

mixing bowl
whisk
metal spoon
knife
4 small ovenproof dishes
oven gloves

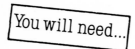

1 Place the egg whites in the mixing bowl and whisk until stiff and glossy. Whisk in half of the sugar until the mixture stands in stiff peaks. Fold in the remaining sugar with a metal spoon (don't stir, just fold!).

2 Slice the Arctic roll into four pieces and place each in an ovenproof dish. Top each with a slice of pineapple.

3 Pile the egg white meringue on top and swirl over the fruit and ice cream to completely cover and enclose.

4 Bake in an oven preheated to hot (230°C, 450°F, Gas Mark 8) for 2-3 minutes until just golden.

5 Remove from the oven and serve at once.

Cat Nap Special

This is really a bedtime drink, but since Henry's Cat cat-naps all day long you can enjoy this milky drink anytime!

200 ml (7 fl oz) milk
2 teaspoons drinking chocolate
2 marshmallows

You will need...

saucepan
whisk
heatproof mug

1 Place the milk in the saucepan and heat until almost boiling.

2 Remove from the heat and whisk in the drinking chocolate until frothy.

3 Carefully pour into the heatproof mug.

4 Float the marshmallows on top and serve at once.

51

Knickerbocker Henry

Henry's Cat adores ice cream, fruit and cake – this is his favourite dessert using all three!

4 slices sponge cake
1 (425-g/15-oz) can mixed fruit salad,
  drained
600 ml (1 pint) ice cream, flavour as liked
150 ml (¼ pint) whipped cream
2 tablespoons chopped nuts
4 glacé cherries

knife
chopping board
spoon
4 tall sundae glasses
ice cream scoop
4 long-handled spoons

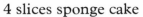

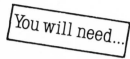

Serves 4

1 Cut the sponge cake into small cubes then spoon evenly into the sundae glasses.

2 Spoon a little of the fruit salad over each.

3 Carefully top each with a scoop of ice cream. Spoon over the remaining fruit salad.

Henry's Cat gets his cream from Farmer Giles...

I'll have extra cream, please. It's always handy to have.

miserable man!

Why was Farmer Giles cross? Henry's Cat had walked on his corn!

4 Using a spoon, top each knickerbocker with a swirl of cream.

5 Sprinkle with the nuts and top each with a cherry. Serve at once with long-handled spoons.

I'm making this one for Farmer Giles...

...maybe it'll bring a smile to his face!

Muddy Fudgy Paws

Henry's Cat is scolded if he leaves muddy paw marks on the floor, but everyone loves him to make these delicious fudgy paw crunchy cakes!

1 tablespoon clear honey
40 g (1½ oz) butter
2 teaspoons cocoa powder
75 g (3 oz) icing sugar
50 g (2 oz) rice cereal

saucepan
spoon
about 10 paper bun cases

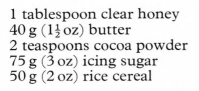

1 Place the honey, butter and cocoa powder in the saucepan. Heat gently until melted and well mixed.

2 Add the icing sugar and mix well.

3 Add the rice cereal and mix well to coat.

4 Carefully spoon into about 10 paper bun cases and leave to set.

Tabby's Striped Treats

As soon as Henry's Cat sees stripes he knows that Tabby Cat is around – he's been fooled by these jelly desserts once or twice!

1 orange jelly tablet
1 (290-g/10½-oz) can mandarin oranges in natural juice
½ ginger cake, cubed
2 (142-g/5-oz) cartons orange or mandarin yogurt

mixing bowl
boiling water
spoon
4 tall dessert glasses

You will need...

Serves 4

"A PEEPING TOM"

1 Make up the jelly in the usual way, following the packet instructions and using the juice from the canned mandarin oranges. Leave to cool.

This time can be best spent putting your paws up...!

2 Mix half of the mandarin oranges with the cake cubes and spoon evenly into the dessert glasses.

3 Pour the cooled jelly evenly over the fruit and cake mixture. Leave tilted in a cool place so that the jelly sets at an angle.

4 Mix the yogurt with the remaining mandarin oranges in a bowl and spoon over the set jelly to top up the glasses. Chill before serving.

How can you tell if an elephant has been in the fridge?
Footprints in the butter!

Little Rabbit Mousses

Henry's Cat often chases the rabbits in the fields but he always catches these in time for tea!

1 packet lime jelly
4 slices frozen mousse, thawed
8 marshmallows
4 chocolate fingers
16 currants
4 pieces glacé cherry

You will need...

Makes 4

mixing bowl
boiling water
spoon
4 serving plates
knife
chopping board

1 Make up the jelly in the usual way, following the packet instructions. Allow to set.

You can do something useful while you're waiting...

2 Place a slice of frozen mousse on each plate and leave to thaw.

EEK!

MOUSSE NOT MOUSE

WOBBLIES JELLY

MEWS of the WORLD

What flies and wobbles at the same time?

3 Place one marshmallow in the centre of each mousse slice for the rabbit's face. Cut the remaining marshmallows in half and use two to make each of the rabbits' 'ears'. Carefully break the chocolate fingers in half and put two side by side to make each of the rabbits' bodies.

4 Press four currants on each face to make the eyes and nose. Press a piece of glacé cherry onto each to make the rabbit's mouth.

Looks like Chris Rabbit...!

5 Scoop the jelly onto a chopping board with a spoon and chop coarsely with a knife. Spoon around the rabbit mousse to make the jelly field. Serve at once.

A jelly-copter!

SIGH!

Nice one Henry's Cat!

59

Henry's Cat's Flap Jacks

These are delicious sweet biscuits that Henry's Cat enjoys with his mid-morning saucer of milk.

100 g (4 oz) butter
75 g (3 oz) golden syrup
75 g (3 oz) soft brown sugar
225 g (8 oz) rolled oats

You will need...

saucepan
wooden spoon
1 (20 × 30-cm / 8 × 12-inch)
  Swiss roll tin
knife
oven gloves
palette knife

Makes about 24

...enough for all the strays in the street!

A Stray cat after my FLAP JACKS...

What do you call a bald stray cat?

Yul Grinner!

HA HA

1 Place the butter, golden syrup and sugar in a saucepan. Stir over a gentle heat until completely melted.

2 Add the oats and stir very well to mix. Spoon onto a greased Swiss roll tin and level the top with a knife.

3 Bake in an oven preheated to moderate (180°C, 350°F, Gas Mark 4) for 30 minutes.

I'll be back later...

4 Leave in the tin for 5 minutes then cut into about 24 finger biscuits with a knife. Leave in the tin until cold.

5 When cold remove the flap jacks with a palette knife. Store in an airtight tin until needed.

I'll leave them to cool off...

HA HA!

Flap Jacks invite trouble!